What Do We Pay For?

Contents

Marilyn J. Salomon

Earning Money

A job can be indoors or outdoors, noisy or quiet, cold or hot. But every job is a way for people to **earn** money.

Construction worker

Geologists

Graphic designer

Buying Goods

We use money to buy the things we need or want. These things are called **goods**.

You can hold them, eat them, play with them, or wear them.

You can even live in them—houses are goods too!

Whenever we buy goods, we make choices.

Is this car the right size for this family? Is the **price** right? If the price is too high, they will choose another car.

Is this computer right for the work
these children and their parents
need to do? Is the price right?

We often choose items that help solve
a problem. This bunk bed saves space.

What problem does this lawn sprinkler help solve?

Buying Services

We also use money to buy **services**. Services are different from goods. You can't wear services, and you can't play with them. But you can't get along without them!

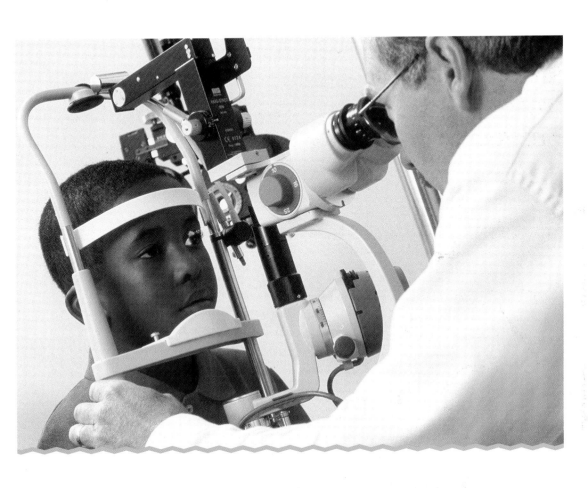

Service workers are trained to do their jobs. We pay these people for their **skills**.

What other service workers help us?

We need services in our **community** too.
We pay **taxes** for these important services.

How would your community be different if these workers were not on the job?

Spending and Saving

Sometimes, what we use to pay for goods and services doesn't look like money. But it has the same **value**.

Here are some of the goods and services we pay for. What other things can you add?

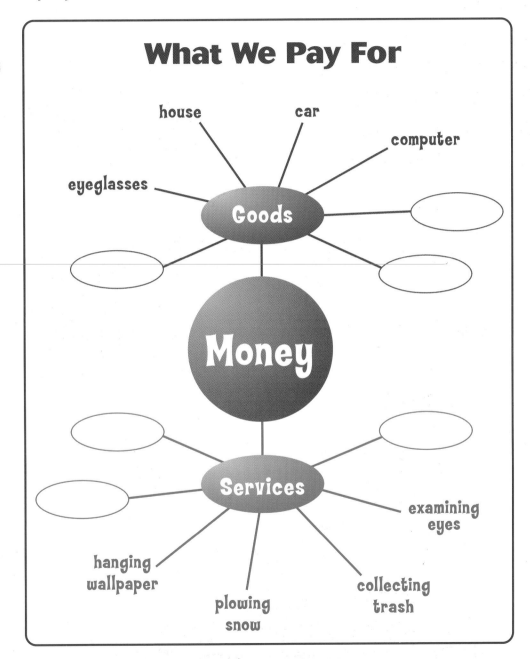

What We Pay For

house
car
computer
eyeglasses

Goods

Money

Services

examining eyes

hanging wallpaper

plowing snow

collecting trash

We use money to pay for many different things. Whatever you choose to spend your money on, remember to **save** some too!